Planes, Trains & Moving Machines

I can draw!

Planes, Trains & Moving Machines

Walter Foster Jr.

Learn to draw flying, locomotive, and heavy-duty machines step by step!

This library edition published in 2015 by Walter Foster Jr.,
an imprint of Quarto Publishing Group USA Inc.
6 Orchard Road, Suite 100
Lake Forest, CA 92630

Artwork © Fleurus Editions, Paris-2014
Published by Walter Foster Jr.,
an imprint of Quarto Publishing Group USA Inc.
All rights reserved. Walter Foster Jr. is trademarked.
Illustrated by Philippe Legendre
Written by Janessa Osle

Distributed in the United States and Canada by
Lerner Publisher Services
241 First Avenue North
Minneapolis, MN 55401 U.S.A.
www.lernerbooks.com

First Library Edition

Library of Congress Cataloging-in-Publication Data

Legendre, Philippe.
  Planes, trains & moving machines / by Philippe Legendre. -- First Library Edition.
     pages cm.
  ISBN 978-1-939581-58-7
1. Motor vehicles in art--Juvenile literature. 2. Drawing--Technique--Juvenile literature. I. Legendre, Philippe, illustrator.
II. Title. III. Title: Planes, trains and moving machines.
  NC825.M64O85 2015
  743'.89629--dc23

                                                                              2014026664

9 8 7 6 5 4 3

Table of Contents

Tools & Materials

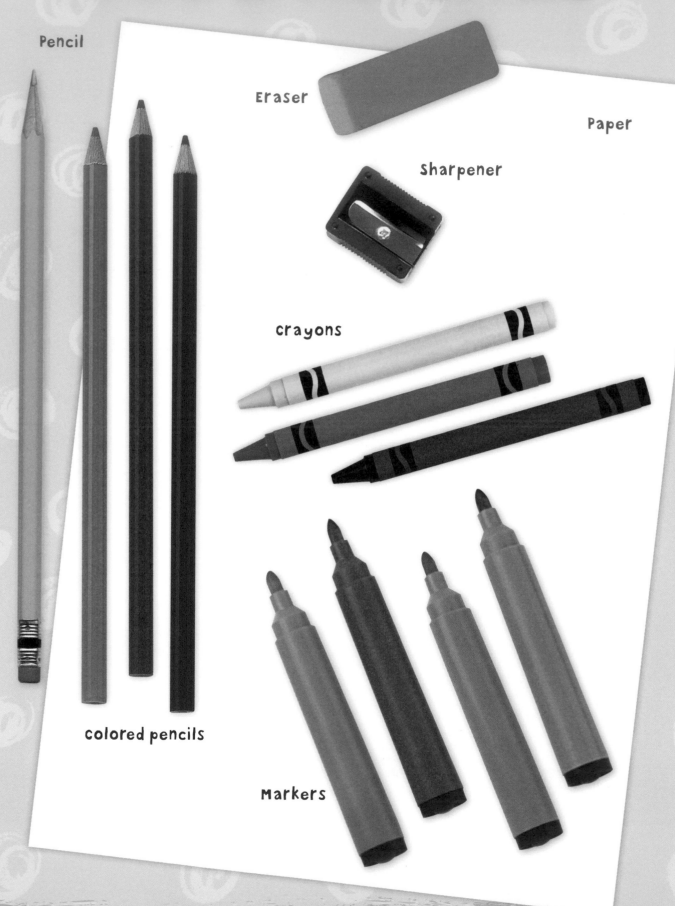

Pencil

Eraser

Paper

Sharpener

crayons

colored pencils

Markers

The Color Wheel

The color wheel shows the relationships between colors. It helps us understand how the different colors relate to and react with one another. It's easy to make your own color wheel!

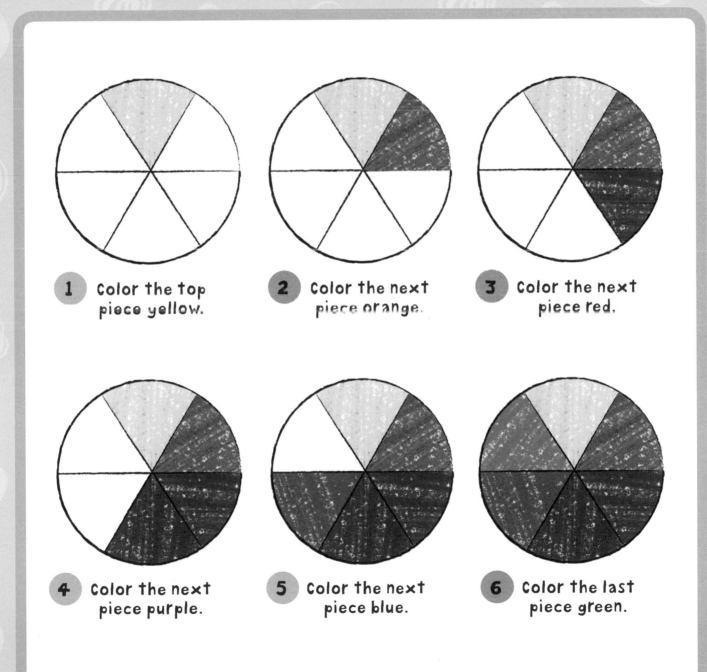

1 Color the top piece yellow.

2 Color the next piece orange.

3 Color the next piece red.

4 Color the next piece purple.

5 Color the next piece blue.

6 Color the last piece green.

Getting Started

Warm up your hand by drawing some squiggles and shapes on a piece of scrap paper.

Draw a square

Draw an oval

Draw a circle

Draw a rectangle

Draw a triangle

If you can draw a few basic shapes, you can draw just about anything!

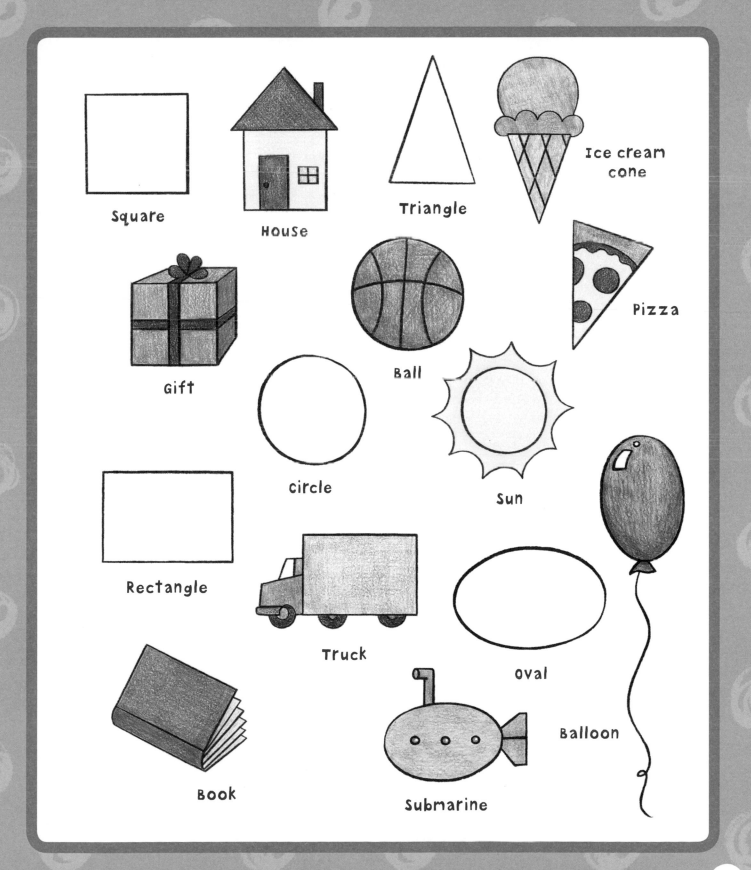

Square

House

Triangle

Ice cream cone

Gift

Ball

Pizza

circle

Sun

Rectangle

Truck

oval

Balloon

Book

Submarine

Military Jet

This type of jet is flown exclusively by military pilots!

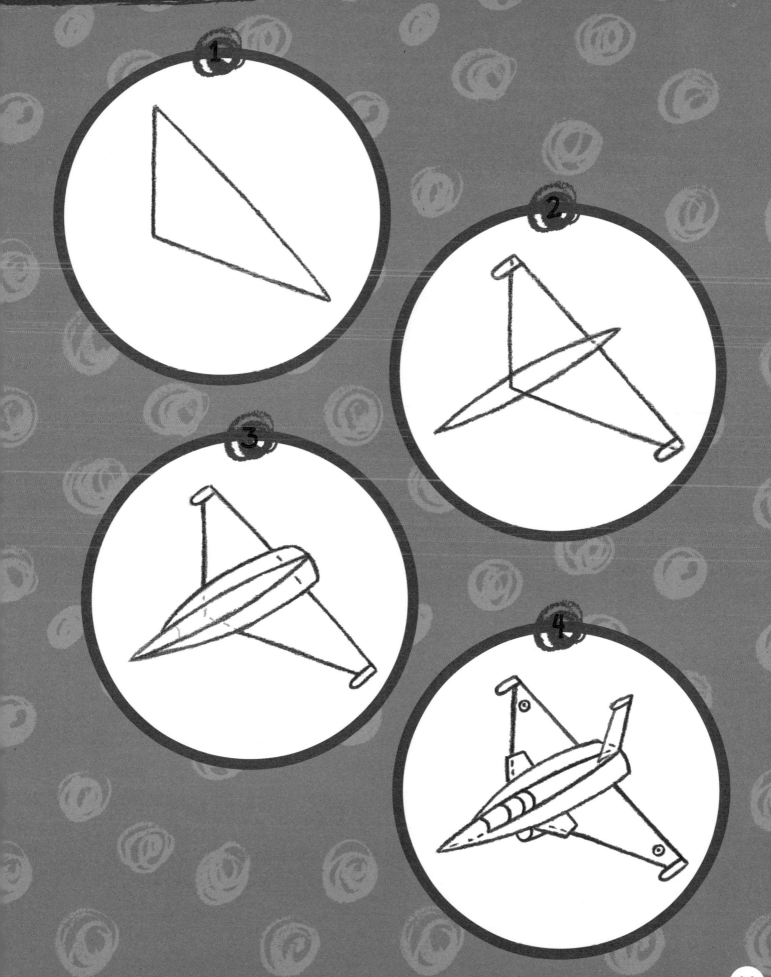

Helicopter

Helicopters can fly in any direction and are used for observation and quick travel.

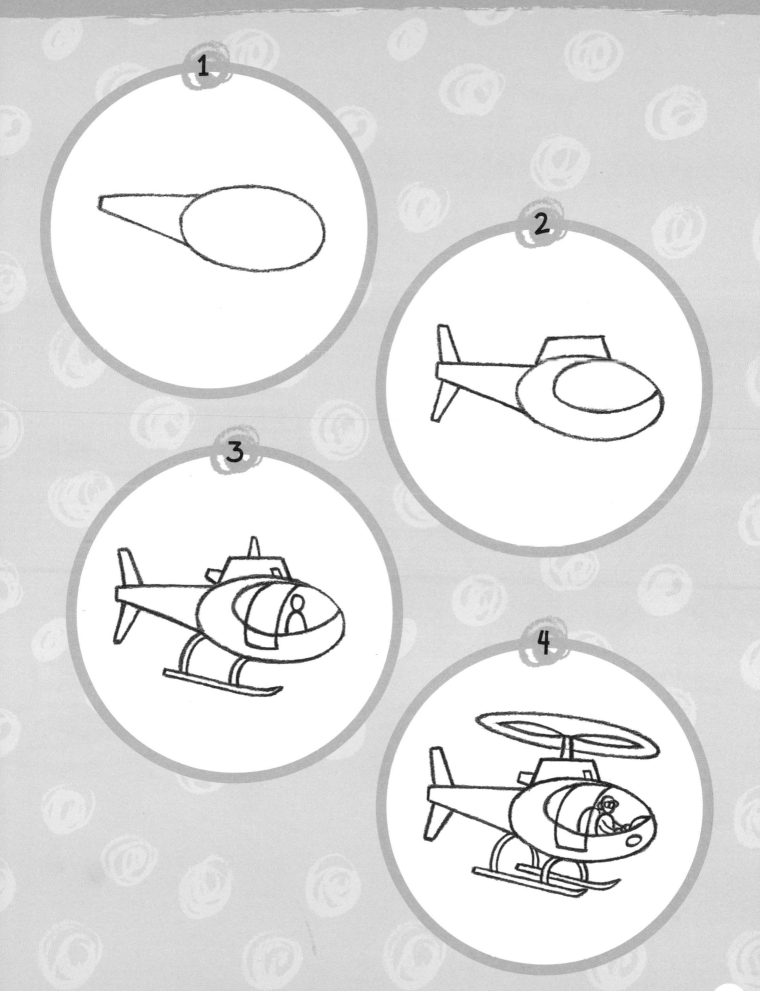

Cargo Plane

This plane is used to transport large packages and supplies.

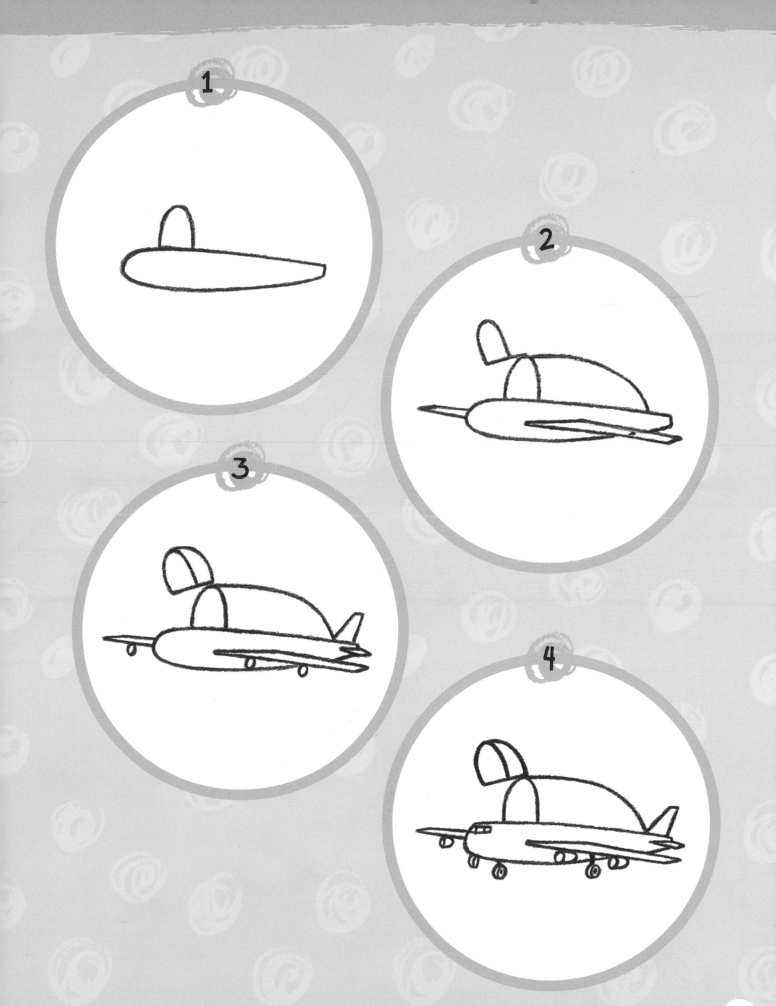

Biplane

This aircraft has two main wings stacked one above the other.

Stealth Aircraft

This aircraft is designed to avoid detection so it can carry out secret missions.

Seaplane

Seaplanes can take off and land on water!

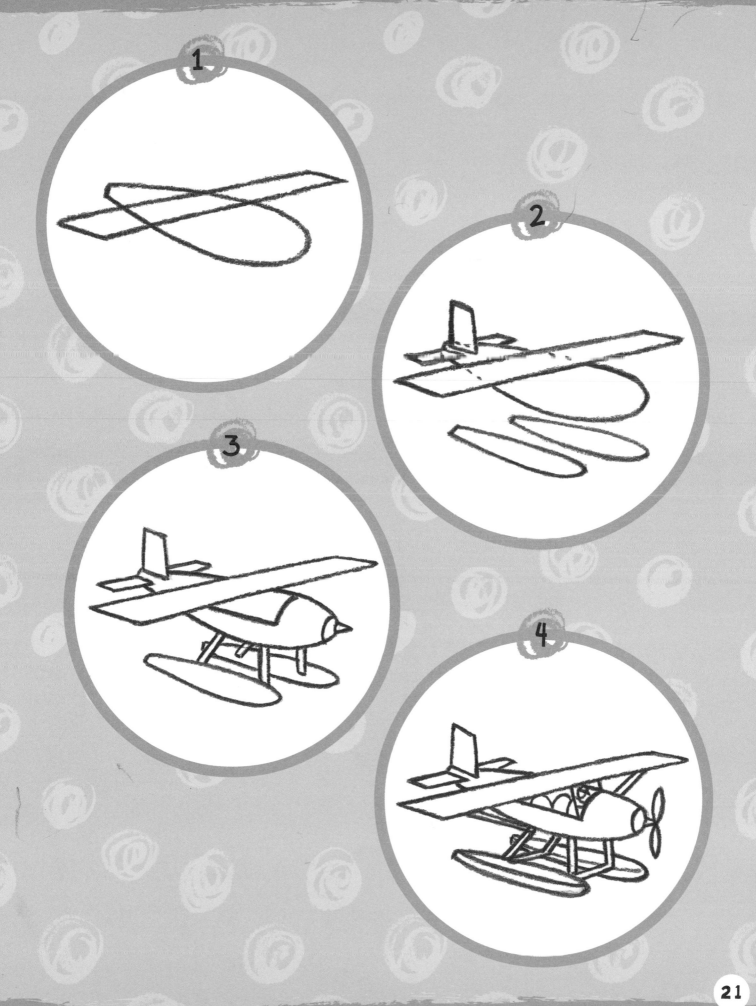

Ultralight Aircraft

This small, compact airplane seats no more than two people.

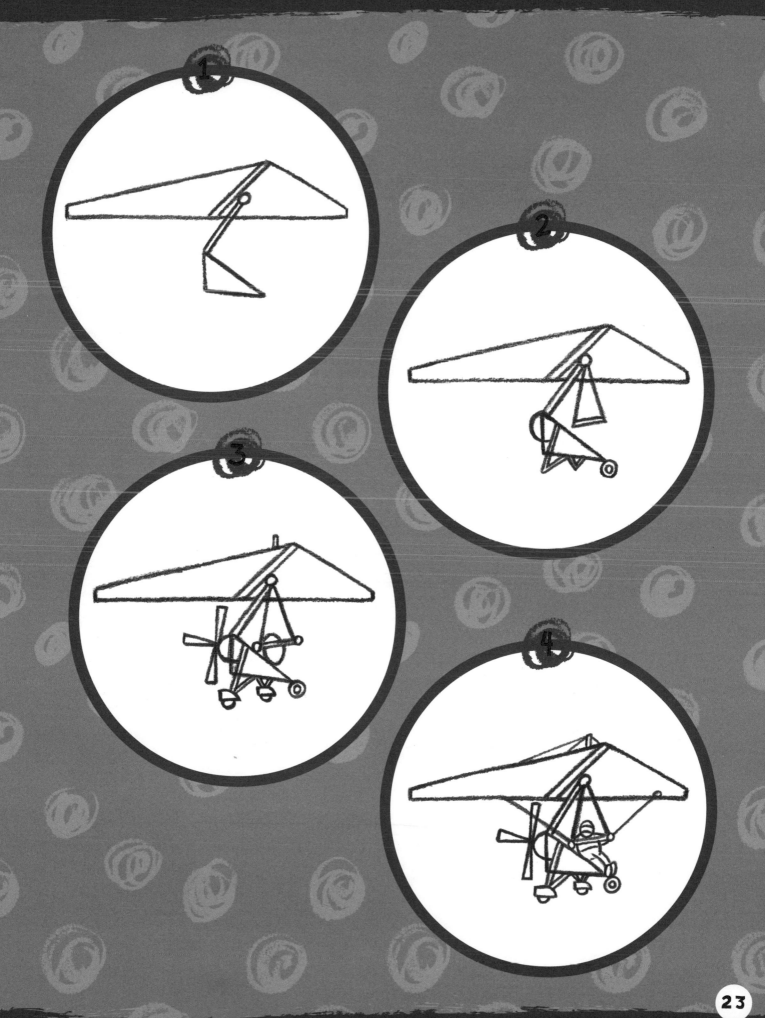

1830s Locomotive

The first American steam locomotive, Tom Thumb, was built in 1830.

Steam Locomotive

This train is fueled by coal, wood, or oil, which produces steam and powers the engine!

Electric Locomotive

This type of train is powered by electricity!

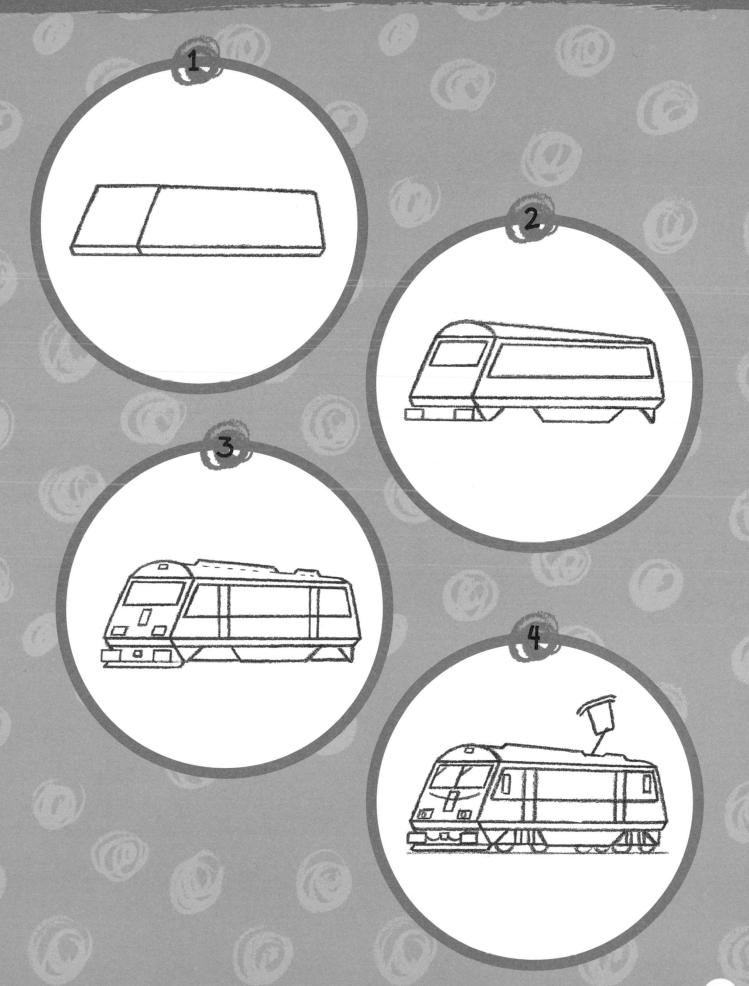

Passenger Car

Also known as a coach, a passenger car carries people aboard a train.

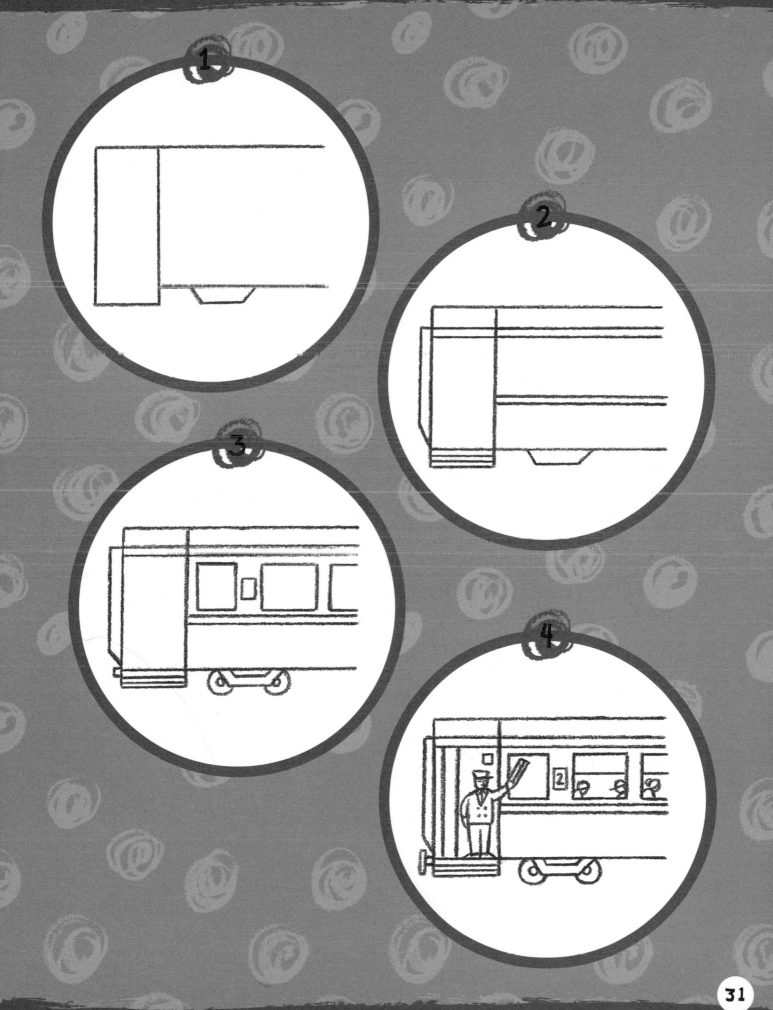

Freight Car

This type of train car transports different types of goods and supplies.

Eurostar

This high-speed railway runs under the English Channel, connecting London with Paris!

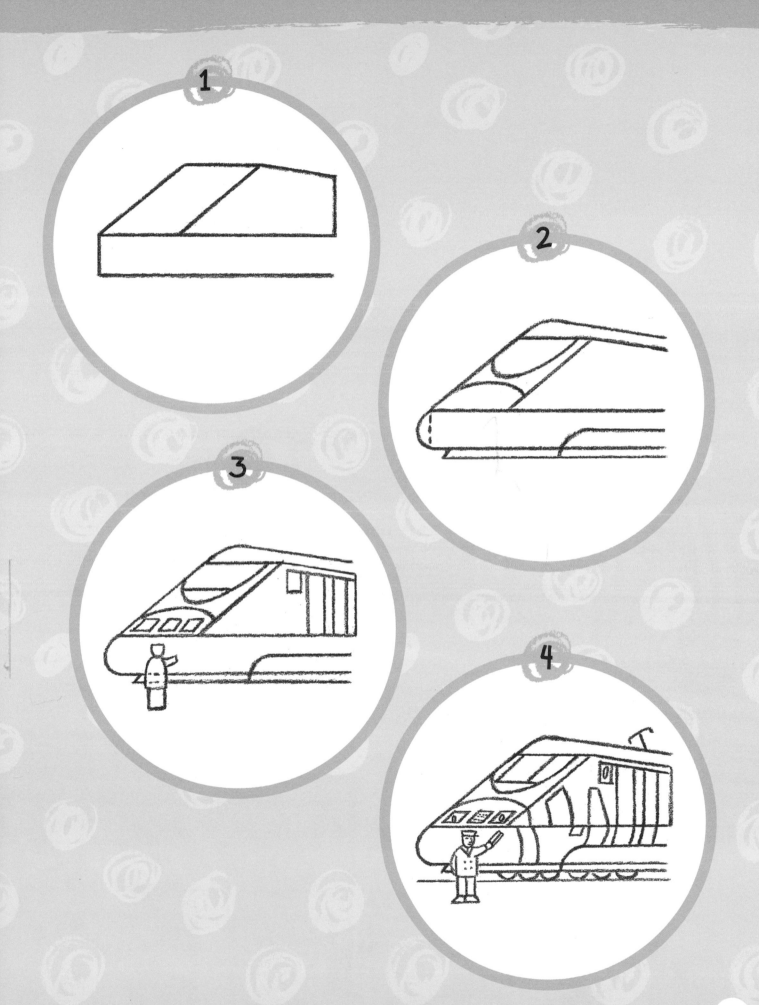

Monorail

A monorail runs on an elevated track, which consists of a single rail.

Tow Truck

This truck is used to transport other vehicles.

Tank Truck

This truck is designed to carry large loads of liquid, such as gasoline and oil.

1

2

3

4

Semi-truck

This huge truck connects to a large trailer that carries food and supplies.

Fire Engine

This powerful vehicle has everything firefighters need, including hoses, ladders, and even water!

Dump Truck

This construction truck has an open bed for transporting and dumping rocks and dirt.

The End